a book about

Lerner Publications (
A Division of Lerner
241 First Avenue No
Minneapolis, Minnesc

Website: www.lerner

The publisher thanks
this book.

Library of Congress

Steiner, Andy.
    Girl power on the
struggles / by Andy
    p.   cm.
    Includes bibliograp
    Summary: Discuss
effect on a girl's spi
    ISBN 0–8225–26
    1. Sports for wom
athletes—United St
adolescence—Unite
discrimination in sp
[1. Sports for wom
discrimination in sp
GV709.18.U6S83
796;.082—dc21

Manufactured in the United
1 2 3 4 5 6 – JR – 05

Le

Lerner Publications Company

ompany
Publishing Group
th
a 55401 U.S.A.

ooks.com

ill Stenburg, who was photographed for the cover of

ataloging-in-Publication Data

playing field : a book about girls, their goals, and their
teiner.

hical references.
s how participation in sports can have a positive
t as well as her body.
0–5 (lib. bdg : alk. paper)
n—United States—Juvenile literature. 2. Women
tes—Juvenile literature. 3. Self-esteem in
l States—Juvenile literature. 4. Sex
rts—United States—Juvenile literature.
n. 2. Self-esteem. 3. Women athletes. 4. Sex
rts.] I. Title.
000
                                           99–28290

a book about girls, their goals, and their struggles

girl power

on the playing field

by Andy Steiner

Lerner Publications Company • Minneapolis

Lerner Publications Company
A Division of Lerner Publishing Group
241 First Avenue North
Minneapolis, Minnesota 55401 U.S.A.

Website: www.lernerbooks.com

The publisher thanks Jill Stenburg, who was photographed for the cover of this book.

Library of Congress Cataloging-in-Publication Data

Steiner, Andy.
    Girl power on the playing field : a book about girls, their goals, and their struggles / by Andy Steiner.
        p.   cm.
    Includes bibliographical references.
    Summary: Discusses how participation in sports can have a positive effect on a girl's spirit as well as her body.
    ISBN 0–8225–2690–5 (lib. bdg : alk. paper)
    1. Sports for women—United States—Juvenile literature. 2. Women athletes—United States—Juvenile literature. 3. Self-esteem in adolescence—United States—Juvenile literature. 4. Sex discrimination in sports—United States—Juvenile literature.
    [1. Sports for women. 2. Self-esteem. 3. Women athletes. 4. Sex discrimination in sports.] I. Title.
    GV709.18.U6S83   2000
    796;.082—dc21   99–28290

Manufactured in the United States of America
1 2 3 4 5 6 – JR – 05 04 03 02 01 00

Contents

chapter one
On Your Mark — 4

chapter two
Why Some Girls Quit — 13

chapter three
Why Some Girls Play — 28

chapter four
Clearing the Obstacles — 42

chapter five
Body Image and Self-defense — 57

chapter six
Trailblazers and Mentors — 65

chapter seven
Games People Play — 78

Resources for Girls — 86
Resources for Parents, Teachers, and Coaches — 92
Index — 95
About the Author — 96

chapter one

On Your Mark

I had a big group of guy friends. Half said girls shouldn't play hockey. The other half said, "Cool." I knew I had to fight for what I believe in. Even though it was tough for a while, I'm really glad I did.

— Katherine, 14

Sound familiar? Katherine tried to get a girls' hockey program started at her school. She found some boys, and even some teachers and parents, resistant. But she stuck to her guns, got the program started, and learned some valuable life lessons. "Trying to get the team started really helped me pick my friends," Katherine says.

Not every girl goes through something like Katherine's experience. But many girls do face pressures, of one kind or another, that can sometimes make it hard to stay involved in sports as they grow older.

For example, here's what happened to Erika, 12. "Once I wanted to play basketball with the boys. Of course I was told I had to play on the girls' team because the boys are too rough," she says. "I told the coach that making the girls play on an all-girl team and boys on an all-boy team seemed like segregation."

In writing this book, I talked to lots of girls like Katherine and Erika. Some I met in person. Others I reached through magazines, newspapers, and organizations such as Girls, Incorporated and Girl Scouts. Ebony, 12, was one of many girls who wrote some interesting thoughts to me. "As a girl it makes me feel bad knowing that some people in the world are looking down on me when I'm play-ing sports," Ebony wrote. "I know what caused it: Us women and girls not doing anything about the situation, being quiet."

Joys and Frustrations

Again and again, girls told me they had both joys and frustrations in sports. "It's good to be a girl in sports today," Erica, 10, wrote, "because girls are getting involved in lots of sports such as softball, track, tennis, and basketball. My frustrations in sports are pressure from boys because they think they are better than girls in sports—but they aren't. It is a kind of prejudice against girls."

The experience of Juliana, 14, was similar: "When we go to gym," she wrote, "the boys say we can't play because we're girls. . . . That makes me feel like I can't play sports."

Busting the
Confidence Busters

At my school, we have lots of boys. When we go to gym, the boys say we can't play because we're girls. Then they say girls can't play sports and make fun of us and it makes us all sad. Then when we mess up, they laugh. I think it's caused by seeing more boys than girls on TV who play sports, and you read more about boys playing sports. That makes me feel like I can't play sports. I should be sitting down watching [the boys].

I told the boys [that girls] can do stuff better sometimes than boys, and sometimes boys do better than girls. We both are people, and girls shouldn't be treated different than boys . . . . Girls can be good at sports or anything that they want.

—Juliana, 14

Tierany, 11, finds "sports are frustrating because some people think girls shouldn't play football. I don't know why. Maybe it's because in football [the players] ram each other. A girl is just as capable of doing what a boy can do on the football field and in any sport," Tierany says. "Now we have softball for girls and women, and they don't have to play with boys and men."

Like Erica and Juliana and Tierany, other girls mentioned that they often face pressure from boys. But teasing by boys is not the whole story. Think about yourself and your friends and how active you are. What do you find? How does that compare to how active you were a few years ago?

The fact is, as many girls move through their preteen and teen years, they become less and less active. A national study by the Centers for Disease Control and Prevention found that the average girl gets twice as much exercise during ninth grade as she does during her senior year in high school!

Here's what happened to another girl, Deb. "I was active in sports in seventh and eighth

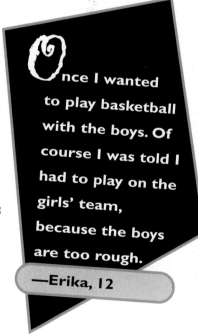

Once I wanted to play basketball with the boys. Of course I was told I had to play on the girls' team, because the boys are too rough.

—Erika, 12

grade," she says. "By the time I got to high school, I didn't do anything. I didn't take gym, and I wasn't in any organized sport. I just lost interest."

Or consider Adrienne, 16. She'd always loved gymnastics, a sport that had given her many skills—and a strong body. Being strong was fine, until Adrienne entered junior high. Then one day she took a close look at her reflection in a mirror. She was shocked to see how big the muscles in her legs had become. "My confidence in myself dropped quite a bit," Adrienne remembers. Soon after, she dropped out of gymnastics.

Holding Your Head High

Confidence—or the lack of it—can play a big role in a girl's life. I remember myself in junior high. I was always picked last for games in gym class. I felt out of place on teams.

Then my mother signed me up for skating lessons. Skating didn't come easily for me either, but this time I stuck with it. I never became an Olympic skater, but I did become a competent skater. As an adult, I feel proud and confident each time I put on a pair of skates. That sliver of confidence in sports led me to my job as someone who writes about—among other things—sports.

Confidence is a key benefit girls can get from sports. "My joys are . . . winning sports games and being all I can be," Erica wrote. "I feel good about being a girl, and I'm proud of myself. All girls should be proud of themselves and play sports whenever they want to."

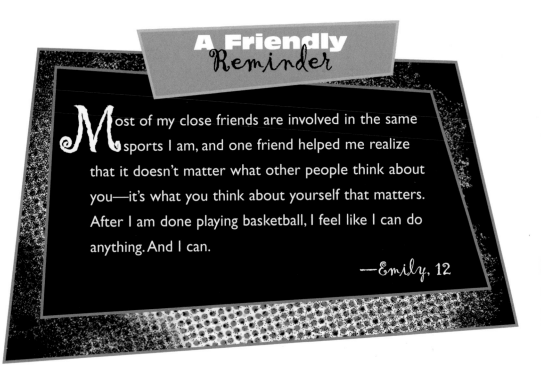

A Friendly Reminder

Most of my close friends are involved in the same sports I am, and one friend helped me realize that it doesn't matter what other people think about you—it's what you think about yourself that matters. After I am done playing basketball, I feel like I can do anything. And I can.

—*Emily,* 12

Other Benefits and Barriers

Did you know that, compared to nonathletes, active girls are more likely to be successful outside athletics? More athletic girls "score well on achievement tests, report high popularity, stay in high school, attend college, and seek a bachelor's degree." That's what a study by the American Association of University Women (AAUW) found.

The Youth Sports Institute of Michigan also studied the benefits of physical activity. It polled 10,000 kids, ages ten to eighteen. Both boys and girls said physical activity helped them have self-confidence, assertiveness, emotional stability, independence, and self-control.

One or another of these benefits always seemed to show up in stories girls told me. "Some girls are better at sports than others," Brittany, 10, wrote. "However, through practice and patience, [any girl] can greatly improve. I am a prime example. . . . In gymnastics, I found it difficult to learn how to do a limbra—a handstand with a backbend and roll." Brittany felt "angry and depressed," she wrote. "But my teacher encouraged me to keep trying. With her help and my hard work, I realized that I can do anything if I put my mind to it."

Clearly, staying active in sports offers lots of benefits to girls. Yet those benefits aren't always available—even to girls who really want them. Rachel Rief was a second grader when her teacher handed out sign-up sheets for a new soccer team. Only the boys got the sheets! Rachel and a friend, Margaret Kowalsky, got the help of Rachel's dad to form their own all-girl team. The team lost every game, Rachel says, "but we had so much fun."

As Rachel and Margaret got older, though, they discovered that many girls were dropping out of soccer. Sports took a back seat to "boys, makeup, and cheerleading," according to Rachel. Rachel and Margaret felt girls needed more opportunities and better role models to keep up their interest in soccer. That belief led them, years later, to found an all-girl program called FUNdamentals Summer Soccer Camp Just-for-Girls.

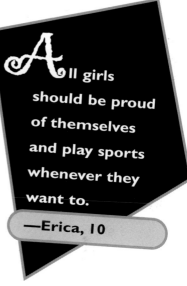

All girls should be proud of themselves and play sports whenever they want to.

—Erica, 10

It seems sports organizations, looks, lack of confidence, teasing by boys, and lack of opportunities can all be barriers girls face in sports. One study, commissioned by Fitness Canada and the Fitness and Amateur Sport Canada Women's Programme, found that barriers to participating in sports exist throughout girls' lives. These barriers range from parents who perpetuate the idea that sports are not feminine to a lack of encouragement in school systems.

Can't Just Sit Around

Here's the good news. Lots of girls shared the ways they leap over these barriers and handle the confidence-busters. Much of what they had to say reveals more about the pressures girls sometimes feel to act in certain ways or to look a certain way. But their comments also show determination to train and to play. Remember Ebony—the girl who thought women and girls are too quiet when it comes to prejudice in sports? "You can't just sit around," she says. "We have to do something, such as talking and taking action in a nonviolent way."

Erika—the girl who wanted to play basketball with the boys—found that speaking up helped her. "I still had to play on the girls' team," she says. "But I felt better after that. . . . You should share your feelings. If you do, you will feel good in the end."

The experiences of people like Erika and Ebony show so much about the ways sports can affect your spirit as well as your body. By learning more about the role that sports can have in your life, you'll learn more about you and the woman you choose to become.

By the time I got to high school, I didn't do anything. I wasn't in any organized sport. I just lost interest.

—Deb, an adult

chapter two

Why Some Girls Quit

> I'm in boys' lacrosse because there is no girls' lacrosse [in my town]. One game . . . I finally got onto the field to play. The kid who was defending me started calling me names and told me not to break a nail.
>
> —*Morgan, in New Moon*

"How Aggravating!" is the name of a column in *New Moon: The Magazine for Girls and Their Dreams.* The column features letters from readers about anything that bugs them. Lots of girls write in about problems they find having to do with sports and physical activities. Often, they describe problems like Morgan's.

We know that, as girls get older, they begin to drop out of sports. Why? We can begin to answer that by traveling back in time and looking at the history of girls in sports.

History *Lesson*

What would you do if someone told you that you couldn't play on a Little League team because you are a girl? What if someone told you that girls shouldn't run, jump, or move too fast?

As recently as a hundred years ago, many teachers and parents expected girls to be "proper" and "ladylike." This meant sitting still as much as possible and avoiding competition and other excitement. And girls certainly shouldn't sweat!

Doctors even said that exercise was bad for a girl's health. In 1905, sports sociologist Dr. G. L. Meylan advised against teaching girls vigorous sports like gymnastics. Too much exercise, he reasoned, could make women look like men. "Of course, we should not care to see our women teachers of physical training . . . approach the masculine type," he said.

Despite such discouragement, many people refused to believe that girls and women should be excluded from sports. These champions of sports equality argued that females had a right to the same sports opportunities that were available to males.

> Of course, we should not care to see our women teachers of physical training . . . approach the masculine type.
>
> —Dr. G. L. Meylan

During World War II, American baseball stars got drafted into the military, just like other American men did. The All American Girls Professional Baseball League was created so that Americans at home could keep enjoying baseball. The young women players were asked to look and act feminine at all times. Their uniforms included short skirts, and they were given lessons in makeup and hairstyling so that they could keep up the proper public image.

League players soon proved, however, that playing a mean ball game was more important than looks. Consider Sophie Kurys. She stole 1,114 bases in nine years of play—an achievement that would have earned her a spot in the Baseball Hall of Fame if she'd been a man.

Not many years after World War II ended, the All American Girls Professional Baseball League folded. In those postwar years, girls and women were expected to be homemakers, not ballplayers.

Through the first half of the twentieth century, there were many women and girl athletes who broke the mold. One was Mildred "Babe" Didrikson Zaharias. Babe (who was also called the "Texas Tomboy") won national fame as a track-and-field star in the 1930s. In addition, she helped found the Ladies Professional Golf Association. Babe ran, jumped, swung, and competed even when others said girls couldn't or shouldn't.

More Milestones

Rayla Allison grew up to be the director of the Women's Professional Fastpitch League, a midwestern softball group founded in 1994. Rayla grew up in the 1960s, when most high schools still provided few sports opportunities for girls. There were plenty of boys' sports teams at Rayla's school, but none for girls. Rayla was a natural athlete who liked to play games with the neighborhood kids. She dreamed of having a career in sports someday. Her parents wanted to encourage her natural abilities. They decided to set up a softball league for girls in their community.

"At first we played with old baseball equipment because we had no money," Rayla remembers. "By the second year, we managed to raise some money and build some softball fields. My parents were the coaches."

By the time Rayla was fourteen, she was re-cruited to play in a women's softball league. The other players were all twenty-six years old or older. After high school, Rayla attended college on an athletic scholarship and played on her college softball team.

Rayla was one of many girls who had to work hard to get athletic opportunities in the past. As late as the early 1970s, boys could join a variety of school teams and compete against other schools. They had coaches and uniforms. Girls often had to make due with poorly funded, understaffed programs.

In some schools, girls' teams were part of an organization called the Girls' Athletic Association (GAA). GAA teams played mostly two sports: They ran short relay races, and they played "girls' rules" basketball. One of the girls' rules was that players could run only three steps at a time before passing the ball! Generally, girls from one school would break up into several GAA teams and scrimmage after school when the boys' teams weren't using the gym.

She can't play because she's a girl.

—Old Saying

On special Saturdays called "Play Days," GAA teams from several different schools would get together to play against one another. Fierce competition was discouraged by GAA guidelines. Players were given plenty of break time for snacks and juice. No fans came to these games. Players wore inexpensive outfits called pinneys. In most schools, the winners never received trophies or letters like the ones the boys could win.

Then along came Maria Pepe. In 1972, she was eleven years old. Maria wanted to play baseball. She tried to join the all-boys Little League team in her neighborhood. Her town did not have a baseball team for girls. Little League officials told Maria that she could not join the team because she was a girl.

Maria refused to listen. She and her parents took the Little League to court. Eventually, a judge ruled that Maria—and other girls—must be allowed to play in Little League.

Maria Pepe's case influenced lawmakers around the nation. On June 23, 1972, Congress passed a law requiring equal athletic opportunities for girls and boys. The law applied to institutions—like public schools—that receive federal funds. This

> My frustrations in sports are pressure from boys, because they think they are better than girls in sports—but they aren't.
>
> —Erica, 10

historic legislation is referred to as Title IX (pronounced Title Nine). Title IX required public schools to offer an equal number of teams for boys and girls. You may not have heard of Title IX. But you should know that without this law, many of the sports opportunities you have might not exist.

Title IX

Here's the actual wording of the 1972 Title IX statute. "No person in the United States shall, on the basis of sex, be excluded from participation in, or denied the benefits of, or be subjected to discrimination under any educational program or activity receiving federal aid."

Thanks to Title IX, women's sports opportunities have grown. In 1996, the U.S. Department of Education reported that about 39 percent of high school athletes were girls. Just 7.5 percent of high school athletes were girls in 1971, the year before Title IX was made law.

When Title IX was passed, budgets in some school districts were tight. Many schools had to cut some of their boys' programs to fund the new teams for girls. The cut in boys' programs caused controversy in some communities. Some people thought boys were being discriminated against in favor of girls. Supporters of Title IX disagreed. Boys had always had more sports opportunities than girls, they said. Boys might need to give up some opportunities for a while until girls' opportunities equaled theirs.

Because of Maria's refusal to accept the notion that girls can't play baseball with boys, an entire world of fast pitches, heavy hits, and stolen bases has opened up for girls. There's even a professional women's baseball team, the Colorado Silver Bullets. The Bullets play against men's teams and sometimes win.

> If you beat a boy at a game, he'll never like you.
>
> —Old Saying

Many women have made milestones in the history of women's sports. In the 1960s, Roberta Gibb Bingay and Katherine Switzer challenged the Boston Marathon's men-only policy. Like Maria, they only wanted equal access to athletic opportunity. Their actions would change women's sports forever. Because of their protest, women began to run in the Boston Marathon in 1972.

The National Federation of State High School Associations reports that track and field has become the second most popular school sport for girls, after basketball. Running is so popular among women and girls that they buy more athletic footwear than men and boys buy.

What Girls *Face*

The history of girls in sports can give us some modern insights. One well-known researcher, Carol Gilligan of Harvard University, talked to hundreds of girls across America. She found that as girls reach puberty—the time when young people's bodies begin to develop adult characteristics—they start to feel less confident than boys feel. By the time a girl is in high school, her self-confidence and self-esteem are considerably lower than they were when she was younger.

Other researchers have found that, at the same age, many girls stop taking part in sports and other organized activities. Boys tend to stay involved in sports as they grow older, the studies concluded.

My joys are . . . winning sports games and being all I can be.
—Erica, 10

Researchers have also found a link between sports and self-confidence. Several studies by the Melpomene Institute, a women's health organization in Minnesota, found that girls who were physically active held on to more confidence as they grew up. Girls who were less active lost more confidence.

In other words, girls drop out of sports at the same time of their lives that their self-confidence droops. Yet staying in sports can help keep confidence high!

The Melpomene Institute found that girls face many obstacles to staying in sports. Here are the top obstacles identified by the Melpomene study:

- The assumption that girls are not good players
- Unfair treatment of girls by the boys they are playing with
- Lack of opportunity
- Inappropriate level of challenge (a sport is too easy or too hard)
- Time conflicts with other activities

That's a heavy list of obstacles. Don't some of them sound like the obstacles girls in earlier times faced? We'll take a look at each of these obstacles. First, though, we need to see how obstacles—past or present—both grow out of damaging gender stereotypes.

Gender *Stereotypes*

"How many times have I heard, 'She can't play because she is a girl'?" asked Anna, 12. "I'm sure many other girls have heard the phrase at least once," Anna says. "I know I have!"

If you've ever heard something like this, then you've experienced a stereotype. A stereotype is an assumption someone makes about you: about who you are, what you like, or what you can do. A stereotype isn't necessarily correct. In fact, people who hold stereotypes about others often don't even know the people they're stereotyping. A person in the United States, for example, might have stereotypes about people in another country.

An assumption that is based on gender—whether a person is a girl or a boy—is a gender stereotype. An example of gender stereotyping shows up in the names given to girls' and women's teams. The "Bears" (a boys' team) could beat the "Bearkittens." The names reflect an assumption about who is tough.

Bambi, a girl who didn't give her age, wrote to me with a vivid description of a stereotype in action. "One day in gym a bunch of macho boys were making fun of a bunch of girls and saying 'Girls can't play sports at all . . . ,'" Bambi wrote. "They also said, 'Girls are just too weak to play sports or anything for that matter.' They kept taunting us for about a week. What I think caused

Because You're a Girl

How many times have I heard, "She can't play because she is a girl"? I'm sure many other girls have heard the phrase at least once. I know I have!

I play several different sports. I play softball, basketball, and volleyball. There are some sports I am decent at but can't play because I am a girl. Football, hockey, and baseball are just a few. People don't offer them to girls no matter how good they are.

Girl athletes have responsibilities. To keep a good image they should have good grades, try their hardest, and have good sportsmanship. When people see you at a game they should think, "Wow, she's a good kid."

These things are all points girls should know to be good, positive athletes. They can be used to improve and show the world that girls and boys are equal and should be treated that way. Maybe then people will be saying, "Sure, she can play because she is a girl."

—Anna, 12

this to happen was a wrongful stereotype that was started a long time ago."

When you were a little kid, you'd never heard "girls can't play sports at all." You hadn't heard that girls aren't supposed to get dirty, to play hard, or to sweat. As you grew older, though, people may have told you to slow down, pull up your socks, fix your hair. These subtle messages about what girls are like can add up to a big message about what a girl is supposed to be.

The worst problem starts when a girl begins to believe the messages and limits herself according to a stereotype. Researchers think this happens to many girls in their preteen years. That's one reason so many girls drop out of sports in those years.

Think back to Adrienne. She saw how big her muscles had become. Then her "confidence in myself dropped quite a bit." "Girls aren't supposed to look muscular" is one message some girls may hear. If a girl believes this stereotype, she gives away her right to be self-confident and physically strong. A stereotype that is limiting or damaging is a bias.

People who used to say girls shouldn't play sports because athletics were bad for them were relying on outdated stereotypes. The truth is, many girls can hit a home run or throw a ball fast. As one put it, "Some boys throw fast, but some girls throw real fast, too!"

What Bambi Learned

Bambi and her friends confronted a group of "macho" boys who were describing the girls' sports skills in a negative way. The girls handled the situation by challenging the boys to a game of volley-ball, which the girls won. From this experience the girls learned a lot of little "minilessons."

- Girls can do anything boys can, sometimes even better
- Boys aren't always as macho as they look or talk
- Never judge a person by what they look like
- Treat everyone the same way you want to be treated
- Treat everyone equally

It's also true that some boys can't catch every ball that comes their way. Others strike out more often than they get on base. Bambi sensed that the boys in her gym class were overestimating their skills compared to the skills of the girls. Bambi and some friends challenged those boys to a volleyball game. "When the game was over, the final score was thirty-two to fifteen in favor of the girls," she says. "We taught them a lesson!"

Like Bambi, many girls find ways to persevere in sports. Let's take a closer look at the obstacles identified by the Melpomene Institute and the gender biases behind them. You'll see how girls are combating gender biases and their confidence-busting effects.

chapter three

Why Some Girls Play

One thing about girls getting involved in sports is that it gives them something else to do rather than hanging out at the local 7-11 or mall.

— *Patricia,* 14

*H*anging out at the mall can be fun. But when a skating star twirls across the ice on TV, the leaps and twists look like—well, more fun! Doing the twirling—or making the basket, or learning a new gymnastics move—is the most exciting of all.

"Girls consistently list 'fun' as their top motivation for sports participation," says Lynn Jaffee, program coordinator for the Melpomene Institute. Since fun is a top motivator, finding the fun in sports may be the your best key to staying physically active.

"Swimming offers endless fun," wrote Meagan to *Zillions* magazine. Meagan compared the variety in swimming to the monotony of lifting weights. "Be it diving tricks and water games or new strokes to master," she explained, "swimming is definitely a cool thing to do on a smoldering hot day."

Everybody's idea of fun is different. *Sports Illustrated for Kids* quoted skysurfer Karen Rambat. Karen jumps out of an airplane with a skyboard (which looks a bit like a snowboard) strapped to her feet. She zooms along on the wind for about a minute before opening her parachute. "Is skysurfing fun?" *Sports Illustrated for Kids* asked her. "You bet!" was her answer. "You feel free and a little scared. . . . I think skysurfing is beautiful."

girls consistently list "fun" as their top motivation for sports participation.

—Lynn Jaffee

Even the dictionary includes the word *pleasure* in its definition of sports. A "sport" can be a team sport or not. It's any physical activity that gets you moving *and* having fun.

Keep It *Fun*

So what sports are the most fun? *Zillions* asked girls and boys to give any sport they could think of a "fun ranking." Kids could only rank a sport if they'd actually tried it. Some fun sports didn't make the *Zillions* list because not enough kids had tried the sport.

For example, boys had tried snorkeling and loved it, so snorkeling was number three in their top ten. Not enough girls had gone snorkeling, so it didn't make their list at all. Lots of girls said, however, that they would like to try this under-water adventure!

But mostly, girls and boys had tried—and loved—a lot of the same sports. Both genders listed downhill skiing as their all-time most fun sport. Girls and boys both liked swimming, with girls ranking it second, boys sixth. Third choice for girls was in-line skating, which was even higher—second—with boys.

Notice anything about these sports? Most can be individual activities. If you read the sports pages of your local paper, you might get the impression that the only sports that count involve large groups of people wearing identical clothing. Sports seem to involve teams, uniforms, and coaches. Obviously, though, when girls name their favorite sports, they often don't think of these things.

T he list comes from *Zillions*. Scores were often nearly the same, so there may be hardly any difference between closely ranked sports. Voters had to have tried the sport to rank it.

Girls' and Boys' Most-Fun Sports

Girls		Boys
#1	Downhill skiing	#1
#2	Swimming	#6
#3	In-line skating	#2
#4	Horseback riding	—
#5	Bike riding	#4
#6	Ice skating	—
#7	Miniature golf	#5
#8	Volleyball	—
#9	Hiking	—
#10	Ping-Pong	#7
—	Snorkeling	#3
—	Basketball	#8
—	Baseball	#9
—	Football	#10

Some girls even stress the importance of not being on a team. Patricia started riding horses when she was in grade school. By the time she was fourteen, she was spending nearly all her spare time at the stable. "I'm competing," she explains, "but not necessarily just to win. . . . Riding isn't like soccer or basketball, where you are playing against someone else to win." Instead, Patricia says, "You're doing it just for yourself."

Like an individual, a team can also play "just for fun" and for individual challenge. The National Junior Lacrosse Association brings kids from all around the country together once a year to play lacrosse, a team sport that's a bit like soccer and hockey. The association wants to keep the focus off competition in its annual tournament. So every team plays the same number of games, and no team is made champion. In fact, officials don't even keep win-loss records!

> I'm competing but not necessarily just to win.
>
> —Patricia, 14

The Thrill of Competition

Following fun, girls list the desire to compete as a reason to do sports, says Lynn Jaffee. Lots of girls I talked to say they *thrive* on competition. For them, there is nothing like the thrill of making

it to the state tournament, winning a race, or set-
ting a record.

Emily loves competing against others. "I love to win," she says. She pushes herself to do her very best every minute she plays a sport. "I like basketball because it's full of action," she says. "I don't like sitting around."

Sports teaches you that you can compete.

—Chris Voelz

Ashley Edstrand was only eight in 1998 when she qualified to race her BMX bike at the BMX world championships. She was asked that year how she felt about going on to the world championships. "I love winning trophies!" she said.

Chris Voelz is the women's athletic director at the University of Minnesota. When Chris was a girl, she played basketball, softball, and sometimes even football with her neighborhood friends. She was a fearless athlete with a competitive spirit who played hard against both boys and girls.

As Chris grew older, other kids sometimes teased her or called her a tomboy. That made her feel bad, of course. But Chris decided to keep playing anyway. Her parents supported her decision, which helped to keep her from giving up. Watch-
ing the athletes in her program at the University of Minnesota compete, Chris cheers them on to

victory. She says a girlhood filled with sports helped her become the athlete and leader she is. "Sports teach you," she says, "that you can compete and win."

The Joy of Teamwork

"One of the most exciting parts of a game, besides playing in it, is standing with the rest of your teammates. Teammates always give each other support. They cheer for you if you do really well one day, but . . . they are there for you if you really mess up or have a bad game," says Tenley, 15. "All the cheers and the signs and the parties show how wonderful team spirit can be."

The satisfaction of playing well as a team ranks high among the reasons that girls do sports. Chris Voelz says that even the shiest girl can learn indispensable social skills by playing on a team. "In team sports, girls learn teamwork, confidence, and direction, not to mention pride and a sense of achievement," she says. "Who can beat that?"

Remember Rayla Allison? Her experiences as both an amateur and as a professional softball player prepared her for her future as one of the women at the helm of a large sports organization. "I learned about strength, determination, and teamwork," Rayla says. "I also learned to be competitive without losing my cool."

Team Player

Being a member of a team is one of the best feelings in the world. It means being with a bunch of girls who, like you, are dedicated to a particular sport and together you are all working toward a common goal. Sometimes the goal isn't even winning— for example, a game in which your team played its best but lost to a better team can be more rewarding than playing a mediocre game but still beating an easier team.

When you are on a team, it doesn't matter what you look like or how you dress. There is nobody to impress. There is no pressure to be really thin or waiflike if you're not naturally that way, because you need a lot of energy and strength to practice or play in games.

—Tenley, 15

The Benefits *of Exercise*

Still another reason girls stay involved in sports is the benefit of exercise. Different sports will condition you in different ways. For example, aerobic activities increase your heart rate and make your heart strong—building your endurance and stamina.

Check Out *the Facts*

Here are some interesting facts about body image, physical activity, and success in life.

- Of girls in fifth through eighth grades, 55 percent said they feel fat or want to lose weight.
- About 22 percent of American women exercise at least twice a week. Only 17 percent of American men exercise as often!
- Roughly 80 percent of the women who are key leaders in the 500 most successful companies in the United States describe themselves as "tomboys" when they were growing up.

Any sport will help you build a strong body and muscles.

And isn't your *strength* a more meaningful measure of your health than the amount of fat on you? Many girls worry about how much they weigh. (Ever heard someone say "I'm so fat!") But girls are supposed to come in different sizes and shapes. There is no ideal weight. Instead of looking at the number of pounds on a scale, consider whether you can carry that loaded backpack all the way home or pump a bike without wheezing.

When Shannon McLinden was in eighth grade, she couldn't even run around her block. She looked in the mirror and saw "fat," even though she weighed 87 pounds. She joined a health club where she could do long, hard workouts to bring her weight down. One day, after a snow sliding party near her home in Minnesota, Shannon collapsed. The "health" routine was too much for her body.

Shannon had to learn how to exercise right. She started jogging short distances, increasing the distance gradually. She added plenty of healthy foods

On same-sex teams, girls can play and try new activities in a safe, uncritical environment.

—Lynn Jaffee

to her diet. In a book Shannon wrote about her experiences, *The Me Nobody Knew,* she tells how sensible exercise and wholesome food gave her unlimited energy. "Amazingly," she wrote, "the rolls of 'fat' I saw on myself in eighth grade have gradually, but healthily, been smoothed from my skin. . . . My face has more color, my hair has more shine, my nails are stronger. I look pretty good!"

"Girls who exercise feel better about their bodies—more confident and sure of themselves," writes Jeanette Gadeberg in her book *Raising Strong Daughters.* "They learn they can rely on their bodies to be there for them."

Reasons to Keep Moving

Self-confidence. Goals. Friends. Good grades. Good health. These are just *a few* more reasons that girls get involved in sports! In colonial and pioneer days, many girls and women did hard physical work like farm chores. They knew about the benefits of athletic activity, if only from their own experiences. Many researchers have conducted studies that support those feelings. The result is that more and more females are pulling on their gear, lacing up their shoes, and enjoying the many benefits of sports.

"Being in sports . . . not only raises girls' self-esteem by teaching them they can get in there and wrestle with the boys," says Chris Voelz, "but also shows girls they don't have to give up being women in order to be athletic. Sports hold you accountable. They teach you to take responsibility, teach you to build a safety net for failure."

Patricia, 14, puts it this way. "People ask me why horseback riding is so important to us riders," she says. "Well, it's not just the riding part. It's everything that's involved in this sport."

The Long Run

Tricia Booker is a freelance writer in Jacksonville, Florida. When Tricia was growing up, she played on her high school's volleyball and basketball teams. Those athletic teen years helped Tricia feel confident as an adult in situations where she might otherwise feel shy.

"I like having the ability to go out and play with the guys," says Tricia. "I'm happy that my body is strong and fit enough to take on any activity, and that makes me feel confident about the rest of my life, too."

For Tricia, sports are a good stress buster. When she's working on a tough story or feeling low, a run helps sort things out. "Nothing looks quite so bad after a three-mile run," she says. "If I go out for a run in the morning, I can face anything during the day."

Why
I Ride

Many people don't know the kind of work and emotions that are put into the care of horses. . . . It makes me feel so good when I can tell everyone, "Yeah, I cleared that three-foot jump course without any flaws." And of course, what rider doesn't love to show off their horse at the shows? It makes them feel proud, and when people feel proud of themselves, it gives them confidence. That is what is the most important thing about sports: confidence and self-esteem.

If you ask my mother, she'll tell you that if I have a bad ride, it affects my whole day. I know that I have been on the verge of tears when I have an off day. But of course it works the other way as well. When I have a terrific lesson or hack (that's exercise), I think about it all day, and it makes me feel good to know that if I can perform that well in my lessons, then I know I can do that well in the shows, too.

—*Patricia, 14*

No matter what your dreams may be, it takes a lot to achieve them. Business executives need leadership skills and patience to direct their companies. Construction workers need to know how to cooperate with one another to build a skyscraper. Truck drivers need self-confidence and practice to maneuver their rigs safely in bad weather. Surgeons need stamina to keep steady during long operations. Participating in sports can help girls develop all of these assets and more.

Girls don't always play sports *today* because of benefits in a *tomorrow* that is way down the road. But it can't hurt to keep them in mind! Sometimes without even realizing it, a girl who plays sports is building a better future for herself.

Here's what one adult, looking back, had to say about her girlhood of sports. "Even now, if I'm looking for a job, I try to envision the confidence I have in sports and apply it to the job," says Kristin, a former high school athlete. "The skills you learn in sports stay with you throughout your life."

chapter four

Clearing the
Obstacles

In school when we have gym we usually play sports like football or field hockey. . . . All my friends, or most of them, just don't try because they are afraid they will be criticized by the boys if they make a mistake.

—*Addie*, 10

It can be frustrating to be told, as some girls are, that just because you're a girl, you can't do something as well as a boy. This is where a "reality check" is needed. The truth is, some of the world's top athletes are women. You can probably think of outstanding athletes you admire—both famous and not so famous. (Maybe you're one of them!)

Recognizing the truth that girls have enormous potential is the first step in addressing a significant obstacle: the bias that girls are not good players.

Girls As *Players*

Jessica, 13, wrote an essay for this book describing this obstacle. "Girls can't play basketball," one boy told her.
"Ha! Ha! Ha!" Jessica answered, "Well, you ain't perfect either." He said, "I don't care, at least I'm better than you." Jessica's response? "Nobody's better than anybody."

> *H*aving boys around changed everything.
> —Patty, an adult

People who tease in a mean way often don't feel good about themselves. Yes, many boys are good sports—fair and respectful. But only one or two bad sports can sometimes take the fun out of a game.

Besides, the idea that "girls are not good players" is not just believed by a few cranks. Consider the way journalists report on women's athletic events. In a book called *Women in Sport: Issues and Controversies,* author Greta L. Cohen points out that sports reporters write and speak differently about female and male athletes. When an athlete is a woman, says Cohen, sportscasters often avoid words like *power, drive,* and *strategy.* Instead, says Cohen, "Positive images of sportswomen are combined with negative suggestions . . . that serve to . . . undercut their performance."

DO YOUR *Own Study*

Want to see for yourself how well sportscasters cover women's sports? You may find good news or bad news. Either way, you'll get good practice in paying careful attention to the media.

Here's just one thing you might try. Select one medium: a nightly newscast that includes sports, a sports magazine, or the sports page of your newspaper. Keep track of how many times male teams or male players are mentioned over a week's time. Also count how many times women's teams or women players are mentioned during that time. Graph the results. How do the numbers compare?

To get an even better idea of how much coverage each gender gets, keep track of how many minutes and seconds are spent discussing each gender's sports (on TV or the radio) or how many inches of space each gets (in a magazine or newspaper).

As an example of her point, Cohen included a story about a male news commentator from a national network at the Winter Olympics. As the commentator watched the women athletes at the beginning of a downhill ski competition, he said: "Once upon a time they were sweet little girls; then something went wrong. They grew up and became downhill skiers."

Role Models

There are many ways to counter the stereotype that girls are not good players. But a strong one is to pay attention to healthy role models. A role model should be someone you admire, someone who provides a great example. Choose a coach or physical education teacher, a mother or an aunt, a professional athlete or a sports writer, or any active woman. "A neighbor who plays broomball every weekend can be a role model," says Lynn Jaffee.

Abby, 12, wrote to *New Moon* magazine about some role models she found. "Last March, I saw the Wisconsin state basketball tournament— the very best girls' high school teams in the state . . . ," she said.

You can't get frustrated.

—Mia Hamm

"I idolized the players so much. They were so good! . . . When I came home, I practiced all the moves, shots, and passes I saw these girls doing."

Unfair Treatment by Boys

Here's an interesting fact that author Helen Cordes dug up. She wrote *Girl Power in the Classroom,* which discusses gender biases in schools. Cordes quotes an Illinois study of playgrounds that showed that 78 percent of the team games on school playgrounds were boys only! These boys-only games took up a lot of space. Barrie Thorne, author of *Gender Play,* found that boys often take up about 10 times more playground space than girls do.

Here's another revealing item. What happens when sports include both boys and girls? According to Lynn Jaffee, "Boys on coed teams dominate play, cut girls out of the action, and ridicule their performance."

Move over guys! To counter the tendency for boys to take up space and sometimes to dominate play, the Melpomene Institute encourages girls to form all-girl teams. "On same-sex teams," says Lynn Jaffee, "girls can play and try new activities in a safe, uncritical environment." On an all-girl team, every girl has an equal opportunity.

Girls often agree. Sarah, 15, wrote, "I think all-girls sports are a wonderful chance for girls to either begin learning a sport they're interested in or enhancing their skills at a sport they have already begun playing."

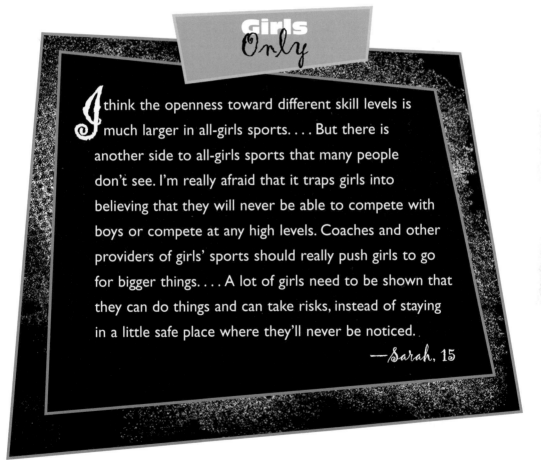

Girls Only

I think the openness toward different skill levels is much larger in all-girls sports. . . . But there is another side to all-girls sports that many people don't see. I'm really afraid that it traps girls into believing that they will never be able to compete with boys or compete at any high levels. Coaches and other providers of girls' sports should really push girls to go for bigger things. . . . A lot of girls need to be shown that they can do things and can take risks, instead of staying in a little safe place where they'll never be noticed.

—*Sarah*, 15

Another way to combat the gender stereotypes of boys is to educate them. Lynn Jaffee suggests asking boys what sports mean to them. Ask them whether girls might deserve the same options.

There's still another way that guys can affect girls in sports. A girl might be more aware of her changing body around guys than she is around other girls. She might feel she has to impress boys by being "feminine"—which all too often can mean "not athletic." Attracting guys is a big goal for some girls. If boys don't think being athletic is attractive, those girls are bound to become less active in sports.

"Having boys around changed everything," Patty, 27, says. "As I started getting older, I got more self-conscious around them, and I'd pull on my sweat pants, and I wouldn't do stuff I could easily do in a gym full of girls." Girls' bodies are changing so much in their teen years. Many girls find they have to pay attention in a new way to how they move. (Thank goodness for sports bras!) All-girl teams can also help ease the feeling of self-consciousness that comes with a girl's changing body shape.

> *Boys on coed teams dominate play, cut girls out of the action, and ridicule their performance.*
>
> —Lynn Jaffee

Lack of *Opportunity*

Thanks to Title IX and other efforts, girls have more opportunities in sports than they once did. Yet the National Coalition for Women and Girls in Education (NCWGE) says there's still a long way to go. In a report card of progress for girls, the NCWGE gave athletics a C, meaning "some progress: some barriers addressed, but more improvement necessary."

What can girls do? Lynn Jaffee advises, "Get active and vocal about creating sports opportunities for girls and women where they're lacking."

That's what Quinn Kitchen did. She strapped on her first pair of hockey skates when she was ten years old. That was the year Quinn—together with her mom, Karen—joined a community hockey league. They competed against other parents and their children. After wobbling a bit and taking a few falls, Quinn and Karen learned to love the sport.

"I call myself a self-made hockey player," Quinn says confidently. "Once I started skating, I couldn't give it up." But Quinn learned that if she wanted to keep playing hockey, she would have to be satisfied with community teams. Her high school, known for its fine boys' hockey program, offered no such team for girls.

This didn't seem fair. When Quinn learned that a group of parents and students had launched a campaign to bring girls' hockey to her school district, she decided to join the fight. Quinn distributed hockey pucks with "Support Girls' Hockey" written on them. She wore her team jersey to school—despite teasing from boys.

> ## My friend wanted to play ice hockey. . . . The coach decided to let her try out for the team, just to prove that girls could not play boy sports. The coach proved that he himself was wrong.
>
> —Makeda, 12

Quinn also gave a speech at a school board meeting. "I have skated for fun for three years," she told them. "This was my first real year of hockey. I enjoy it greatly and know that if I try, I can excel at it and shine with it. A varsity team will be another click of the light, one more step to my goals and a leap in my life."

In the end, the school board approved girls' hockey. Quinn played on the school's first varsity team. Other high schools around her state also set up girls' hockey teams. In Quinn's first year of competition, there were twenty-five girls' teams.

Quinn says the experience of campaigning for sports equity made her stronger and more confident than ever before. In the end, team members won the respect of school administrators, coaches,

Cammi and Karyn, Hockey Trailblazers

Cammi Granato and Karyn Bye—along with their teammates—brought home the gold medal from the 1998 Winter Olympic Games in Nagano, Japan. Both women have been playing hockey since childhood, Cammi in Illinois and Karyn in Wisconsin. As kids, they were forced to compete in boys' leagues, because no girls' leagues existed. In high school—when there were still no girls' leagues—Cammi focused on basketball and soccer. Karyn tried out for the boys' team and won a spot her sophomore year.

College finally gave these two persistent hockey players a chance to compete against women in the sport they love. Both went to college on the East Coast, and both earned Rookie of the Year awards. During the Olympic Games, Cammi was the U.S. team's captain, and Karyn was its leading scorer. Who knows, someday we may see these trailblazers in a women's pro league!

and boy hockey players. "It was a long, uphill battle to get the varsity team," she says. "You learn that you don't fight back by hitting someone. You have to use your brain."

Not every girl is a social activist—somebody who feels comfortable leading the fight for change. You can find a role that's right for you. Just signing up for a sport shows others—teachers, school administrators, and parents—that girls need chances to play.

The Right Level of Challenge

"One school day when I was out for gym class," said Alyssa, 15, "we were asked by our female gym teacher to do push-ups. She asked us [the girls] if we knew how to do girl push-ups. I was very irritated by this question, as I am capable of doing the same push-ups boys can!"

Another girl, Meghann, 14, remembered being asked to play ultimate football. The boys got to use either a Nerf ball or a hard ball. But the P.E. teacher said the girls should use the Nerf ball. That made Meghann mad.

Being underestimated can be infuriating, especially when a person is being judged not on skill but on her gender alone. No matter what a person's talent may be, she still needs support—and training—by a coach to excel at many sports.

The important thing is to find a sport—and a place in which to enjoy it—where your present skills can fit and grow, where you're neither forced to underachieve nor overachieve. "Girls at every level of skill can participate in almost any sport," says Lynn Jaffee. "Find a class or sport that is right for your skill level."

Remember, too, that any age is the right age to start a new sport. Did you know that by age sixteen girls believe they're too old to start a new sport? That's what the Melpomene Institute found. A girl can be an Olympic athlete when she's fourteen. Or she can be a beginner in a new sport at age eighteen. Whatever your present skill level, there's still a lifetime of benefits from any sport ahead of you.

> *I think all-girl sports is a wonderful chance for girls to either begin learning a sport . . . or enhancing their skills.*
>
> —Sarah, 15

Time Conflicts

Here's a tough one. With homework assignments stacked to the top of your locker, chores waiting at home, and club meetings to attend, when does a girl find time to train in a sport—or even just play?

"Even if you are good, sports are challenging," says Anna, 12. "You are always striving to do better than others. Sometimes you compete against other people. To improve and do better, training is necessary. Exercising and practicing is a daily routine. . . . Usually that takes time away from your already busy life."

Anna's words reflect her determination to make time for sports. She believes the many benefits of sports make her efforts more than worthwhile.

Dos and Don'ts

Life is all about rules. We must get up in the morning and go to school. At night we have homework to do and dinner to eat. We're taught to respect our parents and treat our siblings and friends with kindness. These are rules most of us can live by.

But some rules are limiting. Seemingly as old as time, they are based on culture, tradition, and stereotypes. Despite the best efforts of many people, outmoded and limiting rules still exist. Even when we know in our hearts that those rules are silly, we sometimes continue to let them influence the way we live.

Some of those rules are "If you beat a boy at a game, he'll never like you." And "It's better to

cheer for the boys than play hard with the girls."
And "Don't spend too much time playing sports.
Slow down and act like a lady." Rules like these,
based on gender biases, confront many girls as
they reach puberty. Well-meaning teachers,
coaches, parents, and relatives sometimes uninten-
tionally discourage girls' sports participation by
repeating rules learned long ago, when those
adults were growing up.

"My family didn't discourage
me in sports, but my mom
was busy and didn't have
time to attend my basketball
games," says Deb. "She
emphasized academics, and I
got the feeling that sports
weren't that important."

Patricia—the girl who rides
horses—has a different situation from the one Deb
described. "My trainer doesn't
push me," says Patricia, "she
just helps me. . . . My parents
don't push me to be competitive either, but if I wanted to be,
they'd be right there." You can
find adults to support you, no
matter who they may be. And the best supporter—
you—is always nearby.

My parents don't push me to be competitive . . . , but if I wanted to be, they'd be right there.

—Patricia, 14

The Power of You

In the end, the secret to facing gender stereotypes lies within you. Remember that girls are just as good as boys are at sports. Feel free to say so! And then, go out and play and train. Join a team or pursue an individual sport, challenging yourself to be the best athlete you can be.

chapter five

Body Image and Self-defense

Soon after I started eating right I looked
more like my ideal than I had when I
was starving myself. . . . I have unlimited
energy and a skip in my step.
—Shannon McLinden

It felt like it happened overnight. One day, I
noticed that my body looked and felt different. My
waist was slimmer, my hips wider. I was taller, my
feet were bigger, and my breasts were beginning
to develop. I hopped on the bathroom scale and,
for the first time in my life, felt utter dismay.

I felt huge and lumpy. The next day at school I
noticed that I was taller than most of the boys. I
thought, "I stick out like a sore thumb." Because I
felt so big and awkward, I tried to make myself as
small as possible. I slouched. Everything was hap-
pening so fast. I wanted to disappear.

That was my experience, but some girls feel their bodies are changing too slowly. Patty, 27, thought she'd look like a little girl forever. "Mostly it was okay because I was in gymnastics and I was supposed to be small," she says. "But . . . I got tired of being the little one that everybody looked down at."

Growing up is hard to do. Each body develops at its own pace, and no girl follows the "perfect" schedule. For girls, puberty can start at age eight, at eighteen, or anytime in between. Boys, on average, begin puberty two years later than girls do.

In the book *All That She Can Be,* authors Dr. Carol J. Eagle and Carol Colran call girls who grow up quickly the "Fast-Track Girls." Girls who are slower to develop, like Patty, are "Late Bloomers." The authors give girls who develop somewhere in between the nickname "On-Time Girls."

Whatever the age a girl enters puberty, she will

As a rule, girls do not feel very good about their new and different bodies, says Dr. Carol Eagle. "I have never met an adolescent girl between the ages of eleven and fourteen who has said, 'Gee, I love my body. Growing up is fantastic.'"

probably experience a growth spurt that causes significant physical changes in a matter of months. Eagle and Colran describe what happens: "Girls begin to grow at a much more rapid pace. Over the next three to four years, the average girl will become 25 percent taller and will almost double her body weight."

It's no wonder that many girls feel awkward and self-conscious! Remember, it doesn't matter which kind of girl you may be. Whatever the timing of puberty, the feelings that accompany it can naturally be confusing and frustrating. Many grown-up women remember feeling shy, embarrassed, fat, or ugly when their bodies started to change.

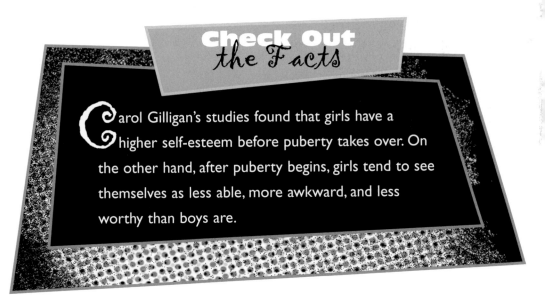

Check Out the Facts

Carol Gilligan's studies found that girls have a higher self-esteem before puberty takes over. On the other hand, after puberty begins, girls tend to see themselves as less able, more awkward, and less worthy than boys are.

Many grown women remember dropping out of sports as girls when the going got tough. For me, it was hard to feel comfortable playing sports when I felt big and klutzy. Sometimes it felt like everybody was staring at me and laughing. Gym was the worst class of the day for me. I dreaded it.

"A girl as young as eleven or twelve may suddenly find that she has to adjust to a strange new body, and for many, it is a difficult adjustment," according to Carol Eagle. "Many girls have confided in me, 'I don't want to change. I want to go back to the way I was.'"

A Thin Line

A common problem that comes along with puberty is a feeling of being fat. At one time or another, if even for an instant, most girls and women have felt fat. Maybe we just ate a large meal, or stepped on the scale, or caught a glance of ourselves in the mirror. For most of us, "fat feelings" go away as quickly as they appear. We shrug our shoulders, shake our heads, and forget about it.

But for some girls, those feelings don't just disappear. A person who feels fat might not want to put on a swimming suit or wear a leotard or be seen jogging. Fat feelings can limit a girl's life.

Fat feelings can cloud a girl's mind and take over her life until she thinks about little else.

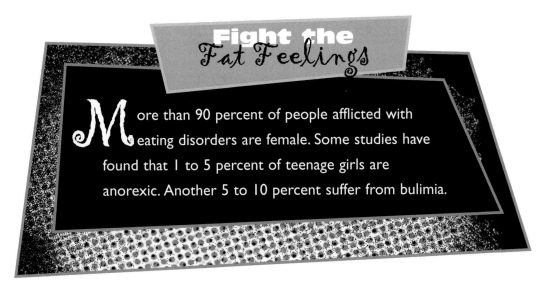

Fight the Fat Feelings

More than 90 percent of people afflicted with eating disorders are female. Some studies have found that 1 to 5 percent of teenage girls are anorexic. Another 5 to 10 percent suffer from bulimia.

When fat feelings take over, a girl can develop an eating disorder. Eating disorders are potentially life-threatening obsessions with weight and weight loss.

The most common eating disorders are anorexia nervosa and bulimia. Anorexia nervosa is self-imposed starvation. A person just doesn't eat and so loses weight. Bulimia refers to secret, binge eating. After bingeing, a person with bulimia makes herself throw up the food or uses laxatives and diuretics (which cause a person's body to void more waste) to cleanse her body of the food. A person with bulimia might also fast—not eat for a while—or exercise excessively to try to lose weight.

Some analysts believe our society's focus on the perfect body drives many girls and women to obsess about their weight. "A girl cannot pick up a magazine without seeing pictures, articles, and recipes that tell her how to lose weight," writes author Jeanette Gadeberg in *Raising Strong Daughters.*

Eating disorders are not uncommon among young women whose bodies are undergoing the changes of puberty. But girl athletes face additional weight pressures. Many sports put an emphasis on body size and even on appearance. Gymnasts, swimmers, ballet dancers, long-distance runners, and figure skaters can focus on "fat" more than they focus on health and strength. The American College of Sports Medicine reports that as many as 62 percent of girls and women in such sports have eating disorders.

Coaches of gymnastics, a sport where thinness is often emphasized, have been known to push girls as young as twelve to cut calories and lose weight. At age fourteen, Kristie Phillips, then an up-and-coming Olympic gymnastics hopeful, took laxatives and diuretics to maintain what she felt was the ideal weight of 92 pounds. Even at that dangerously low weight, Kristie said her coaches considered her fat. "I was called an overstuffed Christmas turkey," she has said. "I felt like a failure because I was fat. These are things that stay with you, maybe forever." Christy Henrich was a skilled gymnast who believed a low weight would help her win gymnastics competitions. She died in 1994 at the age of 22. The cause of her death was multiple organ failure, which was attributed to severe anorexia and bulimia. When Christy died, she weighed 61 pounds.

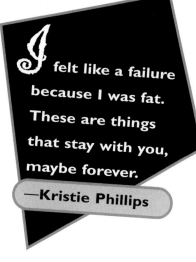

I felt like a failure because I was fat. These are things that stay with you, maybe forever.

—Kristie Phillips

If you or someone you know shows signs of an eating disorder, it is important to get help. Try talking to an adult you trust or calling a hotline for help. There are also support groups and treatment programs for girls with eating disorders. Most girls ultimately triumph over their fat feelings and grow up to be healthy, happy women.

Self-defense

Being physically fit means being familiar with how your body works. It means knowing how to make your body perform at its best. Being in charge of your body makes you feel strong—like you can leap over hurdles, climb mountains, look danger in the eye!

It's important to feel strong. It's even more important to know how to use that strength to your best advantage. Many girls and women are learning martial arts and other methods of self-defense. Knowing how to defend themselves helps them feel confident in a sometimes threatening world.

In *Raising Strong Daughters,* Gadeberg encourages girls to learn self-defense. That way, girls can be "their own best advocate in their personal safety." Girls must take threats to their safety seriously, Gadeberg says. Girls should "demand respect for their body and their space."

Nina Chenault is an expert in Shotokan karate, a martial art. Chenault was the first North American woman to receive a fifth-degree black belt—the highest rank in the sport. Chenault says Shotokan karate has taught her grace and control. "The public perception of karate is that it's violent and aggressive," she says. "But the reality is that it involves calming. If your mind is controlling your body, that's the ideal situation."

Being physically fit means being familiar with how your body works.

—Andy Steiner

chapter six

Trailblazers and Mentors

> Have you ever had a hero? ... Well, I
> do. ... Wilma Rudolph is my hero
> because even though something could
> have stopped her, like being black or
> getting sore all the time, she still...
> made it to the top.
>
> — Rose, 12

Remember Quinn Kitchen? When she fought for a girls' varsity hockey team at her school, she helped girls at other schools pursue their love of hockey, too. Because so many women and girls have grown to love racing across the ice, women's hockey became an Olympic sport at the 1998 Olympic Games. There, the U.S. women's hockey team won all six of its games—and earned the gold medal!

Here are some more stories of athletes who made a difference. Not all of them are famous. Yes, sports superstars can be important role models for younger people. But it's important to know that you can find role models all around you. Remember that even the most glamorous sports superstars were once girls like you. They worried about grades and school. Many felt awkward at times. They couldn't always make their bodies do what they wanted them to do. Some faced tough challenges—just like the women and girls around you.

> *I* always liked hockey too much to stop playing.
>
> —Cammi Granato

Picabo Street, *Skier*

In January 1999, Picabo Street was named 1998 SportsWoman of the Year by the U.S. Olympic Committee (USOC). This honor came after her gold-medal-winning performance in the women's super-giant slalom at the 1998 Olympic Winter Games in Nagano, Japan.

Picabo was a silver medalist in downhill skiing at the 1994 Olympics. In 1995, she became the first American to win a World Cup downhill championship and was named USOC SportsWoman of the Year. She followed that with another World Cup win in 1996 and also won the World Championship in downhill that year. She even starred in a film called *Olympic Glory* released in 1999.

But Picabo wasn't always so successful. Nine years before she had become one of the most highly respected athletes in the country, she was kicked off the U.S. ski team for being out of shape. Picabo also hurt her knee and had to undergo surgery twice. Fighting her way back to Olympic gold wasn't easy, but Picabo stuck to her workouts and realized her dream.

No star athlete starts at the top of her sport. To succeed, most athletes have to struggle to stay motivated, to keep to their exercise routine, to overcome physical difficulties, to stay in top physical shape, or to just plain work hard.

Wilma Rudolph, *Sprinter*

Rose, 12, wrote the following profile of Olympic athlete Wilma Rudolph. "Wilma Rudolph was a sprinter [someone who runs short distances very fast]. She was also the first African-American woman to win three gold medals in a Summer Olympics.

"Wilma was born into a very segregated, poor life. She was the twentieth child in a family of twenty-two children. At age four, Wilma came down with a severe case of polio [a disease that can cripple you for life if it doesn't kill you]. Polio affected her left leg, and she became partially paralyzed. After many years of painful exercises, she was able to walk, run, and play with other children. Then in high school, Wilma became a basketball player. She made twenty-two points in her first varsity game.

> **W**ilma [Rudolph] is my hero. . . . She definitely helped me with my self-esteem in sports.
>
> —Rose, 12

"Then she started training to be a sprinter. At age sixteen, she became a surprise member of the bronze-medal-winning 1956 U.S. Olympic relay team. Wilma continued training and emerged at the 1960 Olympics, winning three gold medals as the fastest woman in the world!

"Wilma is my hero because, even though something could have stopped her . . . , she still pulled through and made it to the top. She definitely helped me with my self-esteem in sports."

Billie Grothe, Wrestler

When Billie Grothe's brother would get nervous before his high school wrestling meets, he'd draft young Billie as a practice opponent. Brother and sister would try out holds, pins, and other maneuvers in the backyard or in the living room.

Eventually Billie's brother went away to college, and Billie thought her wrestling opportunities were over. Girls don't wrestle, at least not at most schools. Beginning with the first Olympic Games, men and boys have wrestled one another. But over the past decade, more and more girls have been joining teams and grappling with both female and male opponents.

Billie turned her interest to other sports. But the wrestling bug wouldn't die. When Billie went to college, she heard that the school was starting a women's wrestling team. She was one of the first people to sign up.

"I've seen many, many matches," she says. "I'm really comfortable with [wrestling]. I like the one-on-one. You have to mentally and physically manipulate them in order to beat them. When you see it so often, it's almost natural to do it yourself."

I'm really comfortable with wrestling. I like the one-on-one.

—Billie Grothe

Billie's college team is one of about twenty-five women's college wrestling teams in the nation. The sport is slowly gaining interest among female athletes. Women's wrestling will become an Olympic sport at the Sydney games in 2000.

Many would-be wrestlers shy away from participating out of fear of injury. Billie is undaunted.

"The guys I've wrestled with have always been bigger than me," she says. "I've learned a lot of

Play Hard, *Play Together*

I play guard on my school's girls' basketball team, the Wildcats. Our team has won two first-place trophies and one second-place trophy in the last two years. My old coaches taught us how to play as a team. "Play hard, play together" was our slogan, and we still follow those words.

Basketball has . . . taught me how to be part of a team. . . . If I hadn't played basketball, I probably wouldn't be the same person I am today. I wouldn't have the same friends, and I wouldn't have the same confidence that I have now. . . . I have always been kind of afraid to go and speak in front of the class, and I think being involved in many sports has helped me conquer that fear.

—*Emily*, 12

defense from that. I like going out there and being aggressive."

Sarah Mergenthaler, Placekicker

The placekicker is one of the most important members of a football team. Just ask Larry Zdilla, coach of the Mustangs, a high school football team in Marlboro, New Jersey. "Placekicking is one of the most difficult jobs in football," he says. "If you miss, you have no one to share the blame with. You can't be afraid of that." The Mustangs' placekicker is strong and confident, with a kick so accurate it makes people stop and look.

It may be easy to think, "So what? Who wants to hear about some boy?" Well, the Mustangs' placekicker is a girl. Her name is Sarah Mergenthaler. She's a member of the girls' soccer team at her school. She tried out for the football team partly because she loves the sport and partly because she admires Kathy Klope. As placekicker for the University of Louisville football

I don't want to be known as "that girl placekicker." I want to be known as Marlboro's kicker.

—Sarah, 16

team, Kathy Klope is the only woman on a National Collegiate Athletic Association (NCAA) Division I-A team. Sarah's male teammates admire her kicking ability. "The players treat me as an equal," she says. "I couldn't be happier."

It's still unusual for a girl to play football. A recent study showed only 328 of 955,000 high school football players were girls. In Sarah's home state of New Jersey, 21,000 kids played football. Only 5 of them were girls.

In one game, Sarah made a thirty-five-yard field goal with only three seconds left in the game. The goal gave the Mustangs a nine to six victory. "Sarah is as good a kicker as I've had in twenty-four years of coaching," says her coach.

Many people would describe Sarah as a trailblazer for girls in sports. Her own description is less lofty. "I don't want to be known as 'that girl placekicker,'" she says. "I want to be known as Marlboro's kicker."

Jackie Joyner-Kersee, Heptathlete

Jackie Joyner-Kersee was a track-and-field champion. Her specialty was the heptathlon, in which an athlete must perform in seven different events—the 100-meter hurdles, the high jump, the shot put, the 200-meter run, the 800-meter run, the long jump, and the javelin throw. Jackie won gold medals at the 1989 and 1992 Olympic Games. Some sports enthusiasts consider her the greatest athlete of all time—male or female.

It may seem that success came easily for Jackie, but it didn't. When she was a girl, she had to work hard to make her dreams a reality. Jackie grew up in East St. Louis, Illinois. Her natural athletic ability was obvious to teachers and coaches at her school and at the community center near her home. Her parents encouraged her to run and jump and play basketball.

By age twelve, Jackie was faster than most of the boys in her neighborhood. She was a star on her local track team. Her parents didn't have enough money to send her away to compete in national track-and-field competitions. To earn money for the trips, Jackie sold candy bars. "I kept saying to myself, 'I've got to work hard, I've got to be successful,'" she remembered.

When Jackie was in high school, she knew she wanted to go to college. To her, part of being successful was getting a college education. Because money was tight in her family,

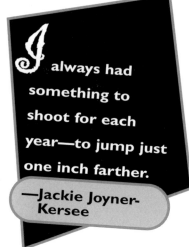

I always had something to shoot for each year—to jump just one inch farther.

—Jackie Joyner-Kersee

Jackie knew she needed an athletic scholarship. She focused on her grades as well as on athletics. When Jackie graduated, she got scholarship offers from many colleges and universities. She accepted one from the University of California at Los Angeles (UCLA). There her track-and-field career took flight.

After Jackie made history with her gold medals, she made lots of money endorsing products for companies. She used some of the money to found the Jackie Joyner-Kersee Community Foundation. The foundation helps young people in poor urban communities. As she said when asked why it was important to her to begin her foundation, "I hope I can inspire someone to take the right path and be successful."

Mia Hamm, *Soccer Player*

Soccer fever swept the United States in the summer of 1999, as fans watched the U.S. women's soccer team win the World Cup against China. Central to the team's success—and its visibility— on and off the field is forward Mia Hamm, the world's all-time leading scorer in international soccer and one of its most reluctant superstars.

Mia grew up in Texas, playing every sport she could, usually against her brothers. Sometimes she'd quit because she didn't want to lose. Her brothers wouldn't let her play unless she finished no matter what. These days her motto is "Never wanting to stop," a slogan that appears in one of Mia's endorsement ads. The words define her philosophy since discovering soccer at the age of seven.

Her early coaches remember her as small but fast. In fact, she was tapped to join the U.S. women's soccer team when she was only fifteen years old. Mia led her college squad to four consecutive NCAA championships and was a member of the 1996 gold-medal-winning Olympic team. As if that's not enough, she's received numerous awards.

The notoriety doesn't much matter to Mia, who sees herself as part of a superbly talented soccer machine. She credits her teammates at every opportunity, admiring their skills while downplaying her own. She is perhaps her own harshest critic and doesn't take her abilities for granted. "I'm no better than a lot of people on the U.S. team. I learn that every day."

I did some good things tonight, but I would like to do more.

—Mia Hamm

Yet Mia also knows that she's a role model and plays her sport with fierce determination and quiet grit. Opponents fear her quickness, speed, and

Athletes
to Watch

Whatever your favorite sports are, you have probably found—or can find—a wonderful role model in that sport to watch. Having a great example can be a big help to any girl. Here are just a few great athletes to keep an eye on.

1. Picabo Street, downhill skier
2. Marion Jones, runner
3. Venus and Serena Williams, tennis players
4. Michelle Kwan, figure skater
5. Jenny Thompson, swimmer
6. Mia Hamm and Julie Foudy, soccer players
7. Cammi Granato and Karyn Bye, hockey players
8. Lisa Fernandez, softball player
9. Christine Witty, speedskater
10. Lisa Leslie, basketball player

uncanny ability to read the goalie and boot the ball. She recently set up The Mia Hamm Foundation to encourage girl athletes of all ages to pursue the sports they love. As Mia has said, "I would not have had the life experiences to date without other pioneers who worked tirelessly to provide opportunities for women in sport . . . . I'm committed to continue [that] progress."

Watching *the Stars*

Ever have a day when you feel as though you don't measure up? Or you just can't do something? Next time, don't hide in your room. Try going for a walk, riding your bike, or jogging around the block instead. You'll build body-confidence and self-confidence. Both can take you a long way in the tough growing up years.

And keep watching those heroes: a superstar you admire, a teacher, a mother, or a friend. Remember many of them have faced financial and physical and emotional barriers. Every girl faces barriers of one kind or another. The determination each girl brings to her sport makes her a hero in her own right.

chapter seven

People Play *Games*

Try a new sport! ... Even a traditionally "male" sport, such as football or hockey, may be right for you.

— *Lynn Jaffee*

Remember how we said that by age sixteen girls believe they're too old to start a new sport? As girls grow up, they conclude that sports are meant for elite athletes—the stars of the local teams or the most dedicated of the professional athletes. Yet you know all the fun and other benefits that sports can bring to your life. Why leave those to the few?

Tara, 15, is an example of a girl who had never done sports until middle school. "It turned out I was good at them," she said. The discovery gave her self-confidence a boost—which made her feel more upbeat about all the things she liked to do.

What sports interest you? Maybe you're on the swim team, but you don't want to limit yourself to that. Maybe you're used to an individual sport, but you're a little uneasy about being part of a team. Maybe you've got some extra time, and you'd like to try out a new sport. These are all good reasons to expand your athletic horizons.

Below are some sports that are easy to begin. Most of them require very little equipment. Almost all are individual sports that you can do alone or with a friend. You've heard of some of these, but some are unusual sports—you may find some surprises! No matter what you're looking for, there's a sport out there that will suit you.

Sport Walking

Sport walking is sometimes called speed walking. It's a bit like regular walking, only faster and with more heel-toe footwork. Sport walkers also take big strides, swinging their arms to build momentum. They often walk long distances. Sport walking is the most popular form of athletic activity among American women.

What you'll need: Sport walkers need very little equipment. All you'll need are a good pair of sneakers and loose-fitting, comfortable clothes like

Girl Power

a T-shirt and sweatpants or shorts. You can sport walk in lots of places: on the running track at your school, on the sidewalk, on a country road, or even in a shopping mall. Stay away from busy traffic.

Benefits: Sport walking is an aerobic activity. It builds muscles and burns calories. Sport walkers also say they feel less stress and have more energy.

How to learn more: There are many books and magazines about sport walking. You'll probably find several at your local library or bookstore.

In-line *Skating*

In-line skates are a cross between roller skates and ice skates.

What you'll need: You'll need a pair of in-line skates, of course. Because this sport involves racing on hard surfaces, you'll also need protective gear. Wear a helmet, elbow pads, wrist guards, and knee pads.

In-line skating is a way to have fun either in a group or by yourself.

—Anna, 13

Benefits: In-line skating builds strength, grace, agility, and muscles and works your cardiovascular system.

How to learn more: One popular book for beginners is *In-Line Skating and Roller Hockey* by Doug Werner.

Running

The name says it all. Running is second nature to most humans. Jogging, as this sport is sometimes called, feels very natural. Joggers run both short and long distances.

What you'll need: As with sport walking, all you need to run are a good pair of running shoes and some comfortable clothes. In the daytime, you can run on a running track, along the sidewalk, or on a country road. You can run in sun or rain. Avoid icy winter days, since you could slip and fall. Also avoid superhot summer days, when you can become overheated.

Benefits: Running is another aerobic activity. Running helps build strength for other aerobic sports such as soccer and basketball.

How to learn more: A good book for beginning runners is *Run, Run Fast!* by George Sullivan. Many community centers and gyms offer running classes that provide tips for jogging safety and fun.

Jazz Dancing

Everybody knows how to dance, right? When you're dancing with your friends, you just move your body to the music. But there are types of modern dance that involve choreography—following prearranged steps. Jazz, or modern, dancing uses new and innovative steps.

What you'll need: Jazz dancers often wear leotards, tights, and soft shoes. Some jazz dancers don't invest in dancing shoes. They prefer to dance barefoot. You can dance alone, but most jazz dancers like to join a group.

Benefits: Who couldn't stand to be a little more graceful? Dancing teaches you how to move your body with both grace and skill. You also learn to be more flexible, strong, and agile.

How to learn more: You can take dance classes almost anywhere, from community centers to private dance schools. If you want to read about the subject, a good book is *Moving from Within* by Alma M. Hawkins. Basic dance skills are also offered on video.

The first time I went on stage, I felt so good because I danced as well as everyone in the group.

—Carrie, 12

Yoga

Yoga is a series of ancient stretching and relaxation exercises. Yoga was developed in India, but people all over the world practice it.

What you'll need: You don't need any equipment to practice yoga. All you need are comfortable clothes and a soft mat or carpeted area. You'll also need a basic instruction book or video.

All That Jazz

𝓙 didn't want to start in the Jazz I class because my little sister was going to be in that class. So I skipped Pre-jazz and Jazz I and went right into Jazz II. It was hard for me, and for a while I didn't like going to classes.

After a few months, I was at the level of the rest of the class. This was a big accomplishment for me, because I had never taken jazz dance before. As I became a better dancer, my classes became more fun. Anyway, if it had been too easy, I wouldn't have liked it as much. As it is now, I'm at the same level as everyone else because I tried my best and worked very hard.

—Carrie, 12

These can usually be checked out at a library or rented from a video store.

Benefits: Many people who practice yoga say

they feel more relaxed. They have increased lung capacity and greater flexibility. Yoga also develops strength and balance.

How to learn more: A good book on yoga basics is *Yoga Is for Me* by Susan Neiburg Jerkl. Local recreation centers often offer yoga classes. Try signing up for a beginner-level class.

Ultimate *Frisbee*

Ultimate Frisbee, a team game based on soccer, is played—naturally—with those famous flying disks most often called Frisbees. Players on each team try to get the disk through the opposing team's goal.

> Ultimate [Frisbee] is just like football, except there's no kicking, no tackling, and much cooler people.
>
> —Ginger, 19

What you'll need: You'll need running shoes and a disk. The game is mostly played on an athletic field, but a big open space in a park would work, too.

Benefits: You'll learn teamwork as well as throwing skill and accuracy.

How to learn more: You can learn the rules of the game yourself by reading a book. A good one is *Frisbee Disk Basics* by Dab Roddick. If you'd like to join an Ultimate league, write to the International Frisbee Disk Association, P.O. Box 970, San Gabriel, CA 91776. The association can tell you about leagues in your area.

Get Going!

Throughout this book, we've heard from teen athletes and ex-teen athletes about the benefits of sports both while you're young and later in life. Being physically active builds self-esteem along with strong bodies, and playing a sport teaches you lessons you'll need when you join the workforce. So think about it. As Ebony said, you can't just sit around waiting for the benefits to come to you!

Resources *for Girls*

Many publications, organizations, and programs can provide information to you if you want to learn more about sports, yourself, and the issues you're facing as you grow up. In fact, it seems every sport has its own website or magazine! Here are just a few of the available resources. The phone numbers with an 800 or an 888 area code are free.

However, you should call a crisis hotline—such as 1-800-4-A-CHILD—if you feel you have a serious problem, including being abused, using drugs or alcohol, being depressed, getting pregnant, or running away from home. The yellow pages of your telephone book lists local resources under "Crisis Intervention." Remember, too, that you can talk to a parent, an older sibling, the parent of a friend, a teacher, or a school counselor.

Organizations—Mentors and Girl Groups

Volunteers at Big Sisters spend time with girls and serve as mentors. Some chapters offer a "Life Choices" program that helps girls make the best decisions for themselves. You can also look in your phone book for a local Big Brothers Big Sisters number.

Big Brothers Big Sisters of America
230 North 13th Street
Philadelphia, PA 19107
(215) 567-7000
www.bbbsa.org

Girls, Incorporated has many local chapters where girls gather for fun and learning.

Girls, Incorporated
30 East 33rd Street
New York, NY 10016
(212) 689-3700
www.girlsinc.org

Girl Scouts go way beyond camping these days and offer lots of fun learning experiences. A contemporary issues program helps girls learn about self-esteem, health issues, good relationships, stress management, and other topics. The national office can help you find a local troop.

Girl Scouts of the USA
420 Fifth Avenue
New York, NY 10018-2702
(800) 223-0624
www.gsusa.org

After-school YWCA clubs include PACT, a peer education program in which girls learn to teach other girls about health and sexuality issues, about how to resist peer pressure, and about how to be a leader, among other programs.

YWCA of the USA
726 Broadway
New York, NY 10003
(800) YWCA-US1
www.ywca.org

Organizations—Health, Sexuality, and Body Changes

The National Eating Disorders Organization (NEDO) offers free information about anorexia, bulimia, and exercise addiction and makes local referrals for treatment.

NEDO
6655 South Yale Avenue
Tulsa, OK 74136
(918) 481-4044
www.laureate.com

You can contact the National Gay and Lesbian Task Force (NGLTF) for a referral to a local support group or organization for lesbian, gay, bisexual, and transgender young people.

NGLTF
1700 Kalorama Road NW
Washington, DC 20009
(202) 332-6483
www.ngltf.org

Planned Parenthood helps with questions about birth control, pregnancy tests, abortion, and sexuality counseling. They can send information. Dialing (800) 230-PLAN automatically connects you with the nearest clinic. Some areas offer a peer education service for girls.

Planned Parenthood Federation of America
810 Seventh Avenue
New York, NY 10019
(800) 829-7732
www.plannedparenthood.org

The Sex Information Education Councils will refer you to local organizations that can help with questions about the body, sex, and pregnancy.

Sex Information Education Councils of the United States
130 West 42nd Street, Suite 350
New York, NY 10036
(212) 819-9770
www.siecus.org

Magazines and Newspapers

Blue Jean, a magazine for older girls, focuses on publishing what young women are "thinking, saying, and doing."

 Blue Jean
 Post Office Box 507
 Victor, NY 14564
 (716) 924-4080
 www.bluejeanmag.com

New Girl Times is a national newspaper for girls. It has "all the news that's fit to empower," along with fiction, puzzles, and poetry.

 New Girl Times
 215 West 84th Street
 New York, NY 10024
 (800) 560-7525

New Moon is a bimonthly magazine that has news and fiction for and about girls. *New Moon* is planned by an editorial board of girls aged nine to fourteen and has lots of things written and drawn by girls.

 New Moon: The Magazine for Girls and Their Dreams
 Post Office Box 3587
 Duluth, MN 55803
 (800) 381-4743
 www.newmoon.org

Sports Illustrated for Women not only has articles on top athletes and teams, but it also gives up-to-date information on new sports, staying healthy, and keeping your motivation.

 Sports Illustrated for Women
 Post Office Box 60-001
 Tampa, FL 33660
 (800) 528-5000
 www.cnnsi.com

Teen Voices is a quarterly magazine written by teen girls about lots of good topics including body image, media stereotyping of girls, racism, sexual abuse, and family relationships. Each issue usually has fiction and poetry, too.

> *Teen Voices*
> Post Office Box 120027
> Boston, MA 02112-0027
> (800) 882-TEEN
> www.teen voices.com

YO!, a quarterly newspaper, is not just for girls, but it has plenty of writing by girls on a wide range of topics important to teens.

> *YO!*
> 450 Mission Street, Suite 204
> San Francisco, CA 94105
> (415) 243-4364

Websites

FeMiNa—at www.femina.com—has a section for girls that includes information on books, careers, games, health, sports, music, technology programs, and links to girls' homepages.

Girl Power—at www.health.org/gpower—has all kinds of subcategories, including a new one on body image, to go along with information on eating right, staying active, and respecting your body.

GirlTech—at www.girltech.com—encourages girls to explore the world of technology. Subcategories include a bulletin board, tech trips, girl views, cool games, and girls in sports.

Girl Zone—at www.girlzone.com—is governed by a teen advisory board and shares information on books, health, and self-image.

Troom—at www.troom.com—offers information on travel, music, issues, and body changes.

Women's Sports Foundation—at www.womenssportsfoundation.org—gives information on how to keep fit, how to stay motivated in sports, and how to find more sports opportunities under Title IX guidelines.

Books

Abner, Allison, and Linda Villarosa. *Finding Our Way: The Teen Girls' Survival Guide.* New York: HarperPerennial, 1996.

Driscoll, Anne. *Girl to Girl: The Real Deal on Being a Girl Today.* Rockport, MA: Element, 1999.

Harlan, Judith. *Girl Talk: Staying Strong, Feeling Good, Sticking Together.* New York: Walker, 1997.

Jukes, Mavis. *It's a Girl Thing: How to Stay Healthy, Safe, and in Charge.* New York: Knopf, 1996.

McCoy, Kathy, and Charles Wibbelsman. *The Teenage Body Book.* New York: Putnam, 1999.

Roehm, Michelle, ed. *Girls Know Best: Advice for Girls from Girls on Just About Everything.* Hillsboro, OR: Beyond Words, 1997.

Sandler. Sara. *Ophelia Speaks: Adolescent Girls Write about Their Search for Self.* New York: HarperCollins, 1999.

Steiner, Andy. *A Sporting Chance: Sports and Gender.* Minneapolis, MN: Lerner Publications Company, 1995.

Resources
for Parents, Teachers, and Coaches

Organizations

The catalog of the American Association of University Women (AAUW) lists publications and videos that encourage girls in nontraditional areas and that give advice on handling issues such as sexual harassment. AAUW also sponsors Sister-to-Sister girls' conferences around the country.

> AAUW
> 1111 16th Street NW
> Washington, DC 20036
> (202) 785-7700
> (call 800 326-AAUW for catalog)
> www.aauw.org

Girls, Incorporated provides a variety of resources to teachers, including Operation SMART, a program that encourages girls in science, math, and technology.

> Girls, Incorporated
> 30 East 33rd Street
> New York, NY 10016
> (212) 689-3700
> www.girlsinc.org

The Melpomene Institute, which addresses women's and girls' health and sports needs, will send information packets on fitness, how girls can gain confidence through sports, and how adults affect girls' body images.

> The Melpomene Institute
> 1010 University Avenue
> St. Paul, MN 55104
> (651) 642-1951
> www.melpomene.org

The National Women's History Project has plenty of information and resources about our foremothers. The organization offers a catalog and has a website.

National Women's History Project
7738 Bell Road
Windsor, CA 95492
(707) 838-6000
www.nwhp.org

The Women's College Coalition has a website—called Expect the Best from a Girl—to visit for resources and tips on helping girls get the most out of school and sports.

Women's College Coalition
125 Michigan Avenue NE
Washington, DC 20017
(202) 234-0443
www.academic.org

The Women's Educational Equity Act (WEEA) will send a free catalog with plenty of resources to promote girls' self-esteem.

WEEA Equity Resource Center
EDC 55 Chapel Street
Newton, MA 02458
(800) 225-3088
www.edc.org/womensequity

Girl Power

Books

Bingham, Mindy. *Things Will Be Different for My Daughter: A Practical Guide to Building Her Self-Esteem and Self-Reliance.* New York: Penguin, 1995.

Eagle, Carol. *All That She Can Be: Helping Your Daughter Achieve Her Full Potential and Maintain Her Self-Esteem during the Critical Years of Adolescence.* New York: Simon & Schuster, 1993.

Gadeberg, Jeanette. *Brave New Girls: Creative Ideas To Help Girls Be Confident, Healthy, and Happy.* Minneapolis, MN: Fairview Press, 1997.

Mann, Judy. *The Difference: Discovering the Hidden Ways We Silence Girls—Finding Alternatives That Can Give Them a Voice.* New York: Warner, 1996.

Odean, Kathleen. *Great Books for Girls: More Than 600 Books to Inspire Today's Girls and Tomorrow's Women.* New York: Ballantine, 1997.

Orenstein, Peggy. *SchoolGirls: Young Women, Self-esteem, and the Confidence Gap.* New York: Bantam Doubleday, 1995.

Pipher, Mary. *Reviving Ophelia: Saving the Selves of Adolescent Girls.* New York: Ballantine, 1995.

Index

All American Girls Professional Baseball League, 15
all-girls sports, 46–48
Allison, Rayla, 16, 34

body changes, 48, 57–59, 60–63. *See also* fat feelings
Bye, Karyn, 51, 76

Chenault, Nina, 64
competition, love of, 32–35, 54–55
confidence busters, 6, 11–12, 22, 25, 60

dropping out of sports, 11, 21, 48, 60

eating disorders, 61–63. *See also* fat feelings
education, importance of, 73–74
exercise addiction, 37, 61
exercise, benefits of, 36–41, 63–64, 80–84

fat feelings, 60–63
frustrations in sports, 5–7

Gadeberg, Jeanette, 38, 62, 64
gender biases, 27, 42, 46
gender stereotypes, 23–25, 48, 54–56
Granato, Cammi, 51, 66, 76
Grothe, Billie, 68–71

Hamm, Mia, 74–77
health and sports, 36–38
history of girls in sports, 13–21

individual sports, 30–31, 79–84
in-line skating, 80–81

Jaffee, Lynn, 28, 46, 48, 49, 53
jazz dancing, 81–82, 83
Joyner-Kersee, Jackie, 72–74

Kitchen, Quinn, 49–50, 52, 65

level of challenge, 52–53

McLinden, Shannon, 37–38
media and sports, 43–45
Melpomene Institute, 22, 27, 53
Mergenthaler, Sarah, 71–72
motivation to stay in sports, 8, 12, 28–39, 41, 78–79

Olympics, 45, 51, 65–69, 73, 75

participation in sports, barriers to, 10–11, 13–14, 17, 18, 22, 49; barriers in school, 11, 16–18, 22, 49
Pepe, Maria, 18, 19
pressure from boys, 5–7, 11, 13, 23–27, 42–43, 46, 48

resources, 86–94; for girls, 86–91; for parents, teachers, and coaches, 92–94
Rief, Rachel, 10–11
role models, 45, 65–77
Rudolph, Wilma, 65, 67–68
running, 21, 81

self-confidence, lack of, 6, 8, 11–12, 21, 25
self-confidence, sports and, 8–12, 21–22, 25, 27, 38, 40–41, 48, 70, 77, 79, 85
self-defense, 63–64
sports, benefits of participating in, 7–10, 12, 36, 38, 41, 53–54, 79–85
sports, opportunities to play in, 18–20, 49–50, 52, 65
sport walking, 79–80
Street, Picabo, 66–67, 76
stress, 39, 80, 84

team sports, 4–5, 10, 30–32, 34–35, 70, 79
time conflicts, 53–54
Title IX, 18–20, 49

ultimate Frisbee, 84–85

Voelz, Chris, 33, 34, 39

yoga, 82–84

Zaharias, Mildred "Babe" Didrickson, 16
Zillions, 29, 30–31

About *the Author*

Andy Steiner is an award-winning journalist who has written many newspaper and magazine articles about girls and sports. She was born and raised in Minnesota. Although she was on the track team in high school, she was a reluctant athlete who learned to enjoy being active as she grew older. Steiner completed a master's degree at the Medill School of Journalism in Evanston, Illinois, then returned to Minnesota and worked first as an editor at a statewide women's newspaper and then as an associate editor at the *Utne Reader*. Steiner is the author of *A Sporting Chance: Sports and Gender*, published by Lerner Publications Company. She lives with her husband in St. Paul.